STAYING ALIVE

INDIANA UNIVERSITY PRESS

Bloomington & London

Staying Alive

DAVID WAGONER

For Herb,
with admiration for
the work and high hopes,

Dave Wagoner
Aug. '66

The poems "Water Music for the Progress of Love in a Life-Raft Down the Sammamish Slough," "Stretching Canvases," "By the Orchard," "The Words," "Leaving Something Behind" (1964); "A Room with a View," "Come Before His Countenance with a Joyful Leaping," "Talking to the Forest," and "Running" (1965) were copyrighted in the respective years shown by *Poetry*. "The Osprey's Nest," "Burying a Weasel," and "Stopping in the Sun" were copyrighted by *Saturday Review* in 1965. The poems "The Fruit of the Tree" (1964), "The Night of the Sad Women" (1964), "The Welcome" (1964), "Staying Alive" (1965), "A Valedictory to Standard Oil of Indiana" and "Night Passage" (1966), copyrighted in the respective years shown by *The New Yorker Magazine*, Inc. "Speech from a Comedy," "House-Hunting," "The Circuit," "Working Against Time," and "Near the End of the Party" were published in 1965 by *Hudson Review*. "The Shooting of John Dillinger Outside the Biograph Theater, July 22, 1934," "Sleeping by a River," and "Looking for Mountain Beavers" appeared in *The Southern Review* in 1966. "Song to Accompany the Bearer of Bad News," "The Draftsmen, 1945," and "Walking in the Snow" were published by *Poetry Northwest* in 1965. "Waiting on the Curb" (1965), and "Morning Song" and "Making Up for a Soul" (1966) were copyrighted by *Northwest Review* in the respective years shown. "An Afternoon on the Ground" and "Revival" appeared in *Choice* in 1966. "Going to Pieces" was published by *Minnesota Review* in 1965. "Fragment for a Bulletin Board" appeared in *Sage*, copyrighted in 1966 by the University of Wyoming. "For the Warming of an Artist's Studio" was published in *Seattle Magazine* in 1964. "After Falling," "Observations at the Outer Edge," "The Poets Agree to be Quiet by the Swamp," and "The Man of the House" appeared in *Five Poets of the Pacific Northwest*, published in 1964 by the University of Washington Press.

*For Jake Hall and William Groeper, who stayed alive,
and for Patt who led me to them,
with love.*

Contents

STAYING ALIVE

The Words

Wind, bird, and tree,
Water, grass, and light:
In half of what I write
Roughly or smoothly
Year by impatient year,
The same six words recur.

I have as many floors
As meadows or rivers,
As much still air as wind
And as many cats in mind
As nests in the branches
To put an end to these.

Instead, I take what is:
The light beats on the stones,
And wind over water shines
Like long grass through the trees,
As I set loose, like birds
In a landscape, the old words.

Staying Alive

Staying alive in the woods is a matter of calming down
At first and deciding whether to wait for rescue,
Trusting to others,
Or simply to start walking and walking in one direction
Till you come out—or something happens to stop you.
By far the safer choice
Is to settle down where you are, and try to make a living
Off the land, camping near water, away from shadows.
Eat no white berries;
Spit out all bitterness. Shooting at anything
Means hiking further and further every day
To hunt survivors;
It may be best to learn what you have to learn without a gun,
Not killing but watching birds and animals go
In and out of shelter
At will. Following their example, build for a whole season:
Facing across the wind in your lean-to,
You may feel wilder,
But nothing, not even you, will have to stay in hiding.
If you have no matches, a stick and a fire-bow
Will keep you warmer,
Or the crystal of your watch, filled with water, held up to
      the sun
Will do the same in time. In case of snow
Drifting toward winter,
Don't try to stay awake through the night, afraid of freezing—
The bottom of your mind knows all about zero;
It will turn you over
And shake you till you waken. If you have trouble sleeping
Even in the best of weather, jumping to follow
With eyes strained to their corners
The unidentifiable noises of the night and feeling
Bears and packs of wolves nuzzling your elbow,
Remember the trappers

Who treated them indifferently and were left alone.
If you hurt yourself, no one will comfort you
Or take your temperature,
So stumbling, wading, and climbing are as dangerous as flying.
But if you decide, at last, you must break through
In spite of all danger,
Think of yourself by time and not by distance, counting
Wherever you're going by how long it takes you;
No other measure
Will bring you safe to nightfall. Follow no streams: they run
Under the ground or fall into wilder country.
Remember the stars
And moss when your mind runs into circles. If it should rain
Or the fog should roll the horizon in around you,
Hold still for hours
Or days if you must, or weeks, for seeing is believing
In the wilderness. And if you find a pathway,
Wheel-rut, or fence-wire,
Retrace it left or right: someone knew where he was going
Once upon a time, and you can follow
Hopefully, somewhere,
Just in case. There may even come, on some uncanny evening,
A time when you're warm and dry, well fed, not thirsty,
Uninjured, without fear,
When nothing, either good or bad, is happening.
This is called staying alive. It's temporary.
What occurs after
Is doubtful. You must always be ready for something to come
        bursting
Through the far edge of a clearing, running toward you,
Grinning from ear to ear
And hoarse with welcome. Or something crossing and hovering
Overhead, as light as air, like a break in the sky,
Wondering what you are.
Here you are face to face with the problem of recognition.
Having no time to make smoke, too much to say,

You should have a mirror
With a tiny hole in the back for better aiming, for reflecting
Whatever disaster you can think of, to show
The way you suffer.
These body signals have universal meaning: If you are lying
Flat on your back with arms outstretched behind you,
You say you require
Emergency treatment; if you are standing erect and holding
Arms horizontal, you mean you are not ready;
If you hold them over
Your head, you want to be picked up. Three of anything
Is a sign of distress. Afterward, if you see
No ropes, no ladders,
No maps or messages falling, no searchlights or trails blazing,
Then, chances are, you should be prepared to burrow
Deep for a deep winter.

The Fruit of the Tree

With a wall and a ditch between us, I watched the gate-legged
    dromedary
Creak open from her sleep and come head-first toward me
As I held out three rust-mottled, tough pears, the color of
    camels.
When I tossed one, she made no move to catch it; whatever they
    eat
Lies still and can wait: the roots and sticks, the scrag-ends
    of brambles.

She straddled, dipping her neck; grey lips and lavender tongue,
Which can choose the best of thorns, thrust the pear to her
    gullet.
Choking, she mouthed it; her ruminating jaw swung up;
Her eyes lashed out. With a groan she crushed it down,
And ecstasy swept her down into the ditch, till her chin

And her pointed, prolonged face sat on the wall. She stared
At me, inventor and founder of pears. I emptied my sack.
She ate them painfully, clumsy with joy, her withers trembling,
Careless of dust on the bitten and dropped halves, ignoring flies,
Losing herself in the pit of her last stomach.

When she gazed at me again, our mouths were both deserted.
I walked away with myself. She watched me disappear,
Then with a rippling trudge went back to her stable
To snort, to browse on hay, to remember my sack forever.
She'd been used to having no pears, but hadn't known it.

Imagine the hostile runners, the biters of burnouses,
Coughers and spitters, whose legs can kick at amazing angles—
Their single humps would carry us willingly over dunes
Through sandstorms and the swirling djinn to the edges of oases
If they, from their waterless, intractable hearts, might stretch
    for pears.

House-Hunting

The wind has twisted the roof from an old house
    And thrown it away,
And no one's going to live there anymore.
    It tempts me:
Why not have weather falling in every room?
    Isn't the sky
As easy to keep up as any ceiling?
    Less flat and steady?
Rain is no heavier, soaking heavy heads,
    Than a long party.
Imagine moonlight for a chandelier,
    Sun through the laundry,
The snow on conversation, leaves in the bed,
    Fog in the library,
Or yourself in a bathtub hoping for the best
    As the clouds go by,
Dressing for dinner according to what comes down
    And not how many.
And at night, to sit indoors would be to lose
    Nothing but privacy
As the crossing stars took time to mark their flight
    Over the mind's eye.

The Shooting of John Dillinger Outside the Biograph Theater, July 22, 1934

Chicago ran a fever of a hundred and one that groggy Sunday.
A reporter fried an egg on a sidewalk; the air looked shaky.
And a hundred thousand people were in the lake like shirts in
    a laundry.
Why was Johnny lonely?
Not because two dozen solid citizens, heat-struck, had keeled
    over backward.
Not because those lawful souls had fallen out of their sockets
    and melted.
But because the sun went down like a lump in a furnace or a
    bull in the Stockyards.
Where was Johnny headed?
Under the Biograph Theater sign that said, "Our Air is
    Refrigerated,"
Past seventeen FBI men and four policemen who stood in
    doorways and sweated.
Johnny sat down in a cold seat to watch Clark Gable get
    electrocuted.
Had Johnny been mistreated?
Yes, but Gable told the D. A. he'd rather fry than be shut up
    forever.
Two women sat by Johnny. One looked sweet, one looked like
    J. Edgar Hoover.
Polly Hamilton made him feel hot, but Anna Sage made him
    shiver.
Was Johnny a good lover?
Yes, but he passed out his share of squeezes and pokes like a
    jittery masher
While Agent Purvis sneaked up and down the aisle like an
    extra usher,
Trying to make sure they wouldn't slip out till the show was
    over.
Was Johnny a fourflusher?

No, not if he knew the game. He got it up or got it back.
But he liked to take snapshots of policemen with his own Kodak,
And once in a while he liked to take them with an automatic.
Why was Johnny frantic?
Because he couldn't take a walk or sit down in a movie
Without being afraid he'd run smack into somebody
Who'd point at his rearranged face and holler, "Johnny!"
Was Johnny ugly?
Yes, because Dr. Wilhelm Loeser had given him a new profile
With a baggy jawline and squint eyes and an erased dimple,
With kangaroo-tendon cheekbones and a gigolo's mustache
     that should've been illegal.
Did Johnny love a girl?
Yes, a good-looking, hard-headed Indian named Billie
     Frechette.
He wanted to marry her and lie down and try to get over it,
But she was locked in jail for giving him first-aid and comfort.
Did Johnny feel hurt?
He felt like breaking a bank or jumping over a railing
Into some panicky teller's cage to shout, "Reach for the
     ceiling!"
Or like kicking some vice president in the bum checks and
     smiling.
What was he really doing?
Going up the aisle with the crowd and into the lobby
With Polly saying, "Would *you* do what Clark done?" And
     Johnny saying, "Maybe."
And Anna saying, "If he'd been smart, he'd of acted like Bing
     Crosby."
Did Johnny look flashy?
Yes, his white-on-white shirt and tie were luminous.
His trousers were creased like knives to the tops of his shoes,
And his yellow straw hat came down to his dark glasses.
Was Johnny suspicious?
Yes, and when Agent Purvis signalled with a trembling cigar,
Johnny ducked left and ran out of the theater,

And innocent Polly and squealing Anna were left nowhere.
Was Johnny a fast runner?
No, but he crouched and scurried past a friendly liquor store
Under the coupled arms of double-daters, under awnings,
    under stars,
To the curb at the mouth of an alley. He hunched there.
Was Johnny a thinker?
No, but he was thinking more or less of Billie Frechette
Who was lost in prison for longer than he could possible wait,
And then it was suddenly too hard to think around a bullet.
Did anyone shoot straight?
Yes, but Mrs. Etta Natalsky fell out from under her picture hat.
Theresa Paulus sprawled on the sidewalk, clutching her left foot.
And both of them groaned loud and long under the streetlight.
Did Johnny like that?
No, but he lay down with those strange women, his face in the
    alley,
One shoe off, cinders in his mouth, his eyelids heavy.
When they shouted questions at him, he talked back to nobody.
Did Johnny lie easy?
Yes, holding his gun and holding his breath as a last trick,
He waited, but when the Agents came close, his breath
    wouldn't work.
Clark Gable walked his last mile; Johnny ran half a block.
Did he run out of luck?
Yes, before he was cool, they had him spread out on dished-in
    marble
In the Cook County Morgue, surrounded by babbling people
With a crime reporter presiding over the head of the table.
Did Johnny have a soul?
Yes, and it was climbing his slippery wind-pipe like a trapped
    burglar.
It was beating the inside of his ribcage, hollering, "Let me out
    of here!"
Maybe it got out, and maybe it just stayed there.
Was Johnny a money-maker?

Yes, and thousands paid 25¢ to see him, mostly women,
And one said, "I wouldn't have come, except he's a moral
     lesson,"
And another, "I'm disappointed. He feels like a dead man."
Did Johnny have a brain?
Yes, and it always worked best through the worst of dangers,
Through flat-footed hammerlocks, through guarded doors,
     around corners,
But it got taken out in the morgue and sold to some doctors.
Could Johnny take orders?
No, but he stayed in the wicker basket carried by six men
Through the bulging crowd to the hearse and let himself be
     locked in,
And he stayed put as it went driving south in a driving rain.
And he didn't get stolen?
No, not even after his old hard-nosed dad refused to sell
The quick-drawing corpse for $10,000 to somebody in a
     carnival.
He figured he'd let *Johnny* decide how to get to Hell.
Did anyone wish him well?
Yes, half of Indiana camped in the family pasture,
And the minister said, "With luck, he could have been
     a minister."
And up the sleeve of his oversized gray suit, Johnny twitched
     a finger.
Does anyone remember?
Everyone still alive. And some dead ones. It was a new kind
     of holiday
With hot and cold drinks and hot and cold tears. They
     planted him in a cemetery
With three unknown vice presidents, Benjamin Harrison, and
     James Whitcomb Riley,
Who never held up anybody.

The Draftsmen, 1945

Given one wall and a roof at a wild angle,
The problem was to find the rest of the house
In Engineering Drawing, to string it along
Its three spread-eagled ninety-degree dimensions
(A line is only a line when it lies flat),
Then trace it up and over, tracking it down
At last to a blunt façade with a shut door.

The whole hot room of us on dunces' stools
Maneuvered compasses and triangles
Over the sliding T-squares and onion skin,
Trying to be on all six sides of a house
At the same time, locking slabs in place
As firmly as the edges of our graves.

We stared at the box like catty-cornered neighbors
Or, losing our perspective, swivelled the earth
Like one-eyed gods till porches spread their wings
And the slant sunlight's isometric waves
Levelled all distance, simply, at a stroke.

And that was that—top, profiles, and front view,
The backside and the rat's collapsible heaven:
Spaces cut out of space like paper dolls
And modelled on a blank interior.

None of us had to draw it inside out,
Sketch in the beds, let smoke through broken windows,
Locate the milkman bleeding in the garden,

Or cross-hatch people running off the paper
Where weather crumpled the uneven corners,

Or knock at the door for any other answers.

The Night of the Sad Women

They are undressing slowly by closed doors,
Unable to find themselves, fading in mirrors
And feeling faint, finding their eyes in time
But seeing, instead, the rooms behind their shoulders

Where nothing is going to work, where photographs
Stand still in frames, arresting other days
When things were turning out. Now turning in,
They are lowering shades and turning off the lights,

But find their fingers lighter than pale linen
At the sinking bedside, seeing their own hands
In front of their faces wavering like gauze,
Then edging away to search in fallen purses.

But they lose touch. In the middle of their rooms
The night begins, the night of the loose threads
Which hang like spiders' lifelines out of seams
To be ravelled to the floor, but not to end.

Water Music for the Progress of Love in a Life-Raft down the Sammamish Slough

Slipping at long last from the shore, we wave
        To no one in a house
With a dismantled chimney, a sprung gate,
        And five bare windows,
And begin this excursion under thorny vines
        Trailing like streamers
Over the mainstream, in our inflated life-raft,
        Bluer and yellower
Than the sky and sun which hold the day together.
        My love, upstream,
Be the eyes behind me, saying yes and no.
        I'm manning the short oars
Which must carry us with the current, or without it,
        Six miles to our pasture.
There go the mallards patched with grey and white
        By their tame fathers;
Down from the leaves the kingfishers branching go
        Raucous under the willows
And out of sight; the star-backed salmon are waiting
        For the rain to rise above us;
And the wind is sending our raft like a water spider
        Skimming over the surface.
We begin our lesson here, our slight slow progress,
        Sitting face to face,
Able to touch our hands or soaking feet
        But not to kiss
As long as we must wait at opposite ends,
        Keeping our balance,
Our spirits cold as the Sammamish mud,
        Our tempers rising
Among the drifts like the last of the rainbows rising
        Through the remaining hours

Till the sun goes out. What have I done to us?
   I offer these strands,
These unromantic strains, unable to give
   Such royal accompaniment
As horns on the Thames or bronze bells on the Nile
   Or the pipes of goatmen,
But here, the goats themselves in the dying reeds,
   The ringing cows
And bullocks on the banks, pausing to stare
   At our confluence
Along the awkward passage to the bridge
   Over love's divisions.
Landing at nightfall, letting the air run out
   Of what constrained us,
We fold it together, crossing stem to stern,
   Search for our eyes,
And reach ourselves, in time, to wake again
   This music from silence.

·

The Poets Agree to be Quiet by the Swamp

They hold their hands over their mouths
And stare at the stretch of water.
What can be said has been said before:
Strokes of light like herons' legs in the cattails,
Mud underneath, frogs lying even deeper.
Therefore, the poets may keep quiet.
But the corners of their mouths grin past their hands.
They stick their elbows out into the evening,
Stoop, and begin the ancient croaking.

The Man of the House

My father, looking for trouble, would find it
On his hands and knees by hammering on walls
Between the joists or drilling through baseboards
Or crawling into the attic where insulation
Lay under the leaks like sleeping-bags.

It would be something simple as a rule
To be ingenious for, in overalls;
And he would kneel beside it, pouring sweat
Down his red cheeks, glad of a useful day
With something wrong unknown to the landlord.

At those odd times when everything seemed to work
All right, suspiciously all right like silence
In concrete shelters, he'd test whatever hung
Over our heads: such afternoons meant ladders,
Nails in the mouth, flashing and shaking roofs.

In safety shoes going down basement stairs,
He'd flick his rewired rearrangement of lights
And chase all shadows into the coalbin
Where they could watch him, blinking at his glare.
If shadows hadn't worked, he would have made them.

With hands turning to horn against the stone
He'd think on all fours, hunch as if to drink
If his cold chisel broke the cold foundation
And brought dark water pulsing out of clay.
Wrenching at rows of pipes like his cage-bars,

He made them creak in sockets and give way,
But rammed them back, putting his house in order.
Moonlight or rain, after the evening paper,
His mouth lay open under the perfect plaster
To catch the first sweet drop, but none came down.

[25]

For the Warming of an Artist's Studio

The previous tenant, running out of business,
Bolted the back door,
Blew out the fuses, sprang the toilet trap,
Unscrewed the hardware,
And didn't leave a trace of his side-kicks—
No cold cashier
Behind the hole in the window saying No,
And no go-getter
Coughing to break the gathering punch-line
At the water-cooler.
Tonight, we'll drink to him. He left the ceiling,
The best part of the floor,
And enough strength in the walls to take the weight
Of an easel's crossbar
On which to float some stock in an enterprise
Also going under
Eventually after going upside-down,
Slantwise and haywire,
But never simply crossing into the red
Like a line in a ledger.
Here goes an artist after a businessman
Not as a panhandler
But, following him through rundown neighborhoods
And making over
The empty premises at the end of his line,
As a silent partner.

Waiting on the Curb

(Death: *"Everyman*, stand still.")

Stalled by the traffic, waiting for the light
And giving a little at the knees, I stand
As still as others tied up in their shoes.
Looking ahead, my eyes switch out of sight,
Commemorating death by doing nothing
And needing a signal to get over it.

Behind my packages, I sweat it out,
Having already memorized the corner—
The fireplug, street-sign, waste-can, cracked cement
With which our city civilizes dirt—
And, feeling cornered, shuffle to keep warm,
Knowing it's useless now to plant my feet.

Ahead of me, all out from under arrest
And rushing suddenly over the jammed street,
The others hurry off to make up time;
But losing this moment, Death, I wait for you
To let me go. My disobedient body
Clings to my spine like a drunk to a lamppost.

Night Passage

The lights are going on over the water.
Over the ridge of the disappearing island
Headlights rise and fall like the ledge of the sun,
And starlight shiftier than eyes
Across the headland flashes the end of day.

Out of the houses and the fading woods,
On the water (scarlet
For rocks and the glimmering starboard landfall)
From the depths, the burning creatures come,
Their luminous slow heads touching the night.

Lights coming on in the dark look out of holes
At others burnt to sleep in the distance,
My mind, going out among them, going out.

By the Orchard

Rushing through leaves, they fall
Down, abruptly down
To the ground, bumping the branches,
The windfall apples falling
Yellow into the long grass and lying
Where they have fallen
In the tree's shadow, the shades
Of their soft bruises sinking, opening wide
Mouths to the mouths of creatures
Who like the sun are falling
To flicker, to worm's end under
Themselves, the hatch of moons.

Going to Pieces

Pull yourself together, pal.
—advice from a stranger

Those marionette-show skeletons can do it
Suddenly, after their skulls have been
Alone in the rafters, after their wishbones
Have fluttered in the wings, leaving the feet onstage
To hoof it solo: they pull themselves together,
Bring everything back and thread it on their spines.

But looking around and seeing other people
Coming apart at parties, breaking up
And catching their own laughter in both hands,
Or crossing the lawn and throwing up their spirits
Like voice-balloons in funnies, touching noses
In bedroom mirrors, one after another,
I figure something can be said for it:
Maybe some people break in better halves
Or some of the parts are greater than the whole.

Pal, take a look around: a heap of coats
Discarded in one spot like empty skins;
Under the tables enough shoes and gloves,
Enough loose hair, saliva, and fingernails
To conjure bodies off a hundred souls.
Now I'll tell *you* one: the palolo worms,
One night a year at the bottom of the sea,
Back halfway out of the burrows where they spend
Long lives; their tails turn luminous, twist free,
And all by themselves swim up to the surface,
Joining with millions of other detached tails;
The sea in a writhing mass lies white for miles
Under a gibbous moon; the bright halves die
And float away like scraps after a party,
But leave behind their larvae, set for life.

[29]

Meanwhile, the old ones, steady in their holes,
Can go about their business, fanning food
Into their sleek, uninterrupted gullets.
Think of them there, pal, chewing the ocean,
Staying alive by going to pieces.

Stretching Canvases

By the last of the light, I pull
Over firm stretcher-bars
The ends of the last canvas
You wanted, miter the corners
Like sheets on a guest-bed,
And staple them on tight.
Stark white, three in a row
Are leaning on our house
To catch at the sunset.
From their surfaces, the stream
Of the undivided spectrum—
The whole palette of light—
Has put out both my eyes.
Good luck, my darling.
I can't see a thing.
My hammer flustered crows
All afternoon, kept jays
Out of the hazel trees.
I'm an aimless carpenter,
And now it's going to be winter
By the rule of this blue thumb.
We need storm-windows
In frames exactly like these.
Good luck to the canvas
Under the boxer's back
And the sail over the circus;
And good luck, facing you,
To the three against the wall
Which may be windows yet.
Keeping the storms in mind
And brushing the sky light
Like the stubble of the wind,
Look through, darling, look through.

The Welcome

For leagues the bunting rose on telephone wires,
And we made way like gates, giving away
Everything handy, gingering old horses
And pressing back as plastered as posters
Against the shop-fronts, spilling their bargains.
Balloons blew wholesale out of the mouths of tubas,
Billboards collapsed on multicolored hams,
And we waited. His lunch lay thawed in restaurants,
His cushions plumped, the girls asleep in cakes,
The corks already popped out of his magnums.
Our faces, all one way, went on and off
Like blinkers down the deserted lanes of the street.
Slowly the peach and lavender gulls stopped flying.

And he arrived on the wrong side of town
With no doors sighing open, no rushing lipstick,
And no quick squeezes for the quick or the dead.
Jaywalking over rails and safety-islands,
Through lawns and alleys, bumping barbecues
And shuffling straight through hedges and ash piles,
Trespassing yards with dogs dogging his heels,
Through summer mulch, the vee's of broken clotheslines
Following him like geese over our fences,
He slipped into the vacant heart of the city
And out the other side without a word.

Revival

(for Richard Hugo)

When Brother Jessen showed the tawny spot
On the carpet where a man threw up a demon,
He had another man by the ear
Beside the rose-covered plastic cross. He shouted
Into that ear a dozen times in a row,
"I curse you, Demon, in the name of Jesus!"
Some of his flock clapped hands. He knelt and sweated.
"They can try skating and wienie roasts," he said,
"But that don't keep the kids out of lovers' lane."
He pointed at me. "You don't believe in demons."

Next door, they were chasing some with double shots,
And the wind was up, and it was one of those nights
When it's hard to breathe
And you can't sit still or talk, when your eyes focus
On all disjointed scraps shoved into corners,
And something's going to happen. People feel fine,
Brother Jessen says, if they can lose their demons.
They wash in showers of everlasting dew
Which is the sweat of angels sick for men.

The demon has names, he told me, like Rebellion,
And it won't submit, it wants a cup of coffee,
Wants to go for a walk, and like as not
Turns up in Hell. Hugo, if you and I,
Having been cursed by some tough guy like Jesus,
Were to lose that wild, squat, bloody, grinning demon
Locked in the pit of our respective guts,
Whose fork has pitched us, flattened us to walls,
Left us in alleys where the moon smells dead,
Or jerked us out of the arms of our wives to write
Something like this, we'd sprawl flat on the floor,
A couple of tame spots at a revival.

Let's save a little sweat for the bad guys
Who can't keep out of lovers' lane for a minute,
Who, when they trip, will lie there in the rut
For old time's sake, rebellious as all Hell,
Croaking forever, loving the hard way.

Stopping in the Sun

On the long slope of the dune,
Stopping in the sun,
I watch the wind heave ribs high in the sand
Among the pines and starweed,
Then spill its shoulder down to a gray cove.

My footprints, all but the final one,
Have been wiped out as cleanly as lost clues.
Now, even the last floats up at the heel,
Goes shallow along the sole,
And turns as light as the pacing of sunlight.

And nothing will save the pair under my shoes.
A raven coasts at the crest,
The ancient joker burnt as black
As a flaw in space. I drift slowly uphill
Against the crosswind lifting us together.

Talking to the Forest

"When we can understand animals, we will know the
change is halfway. When we can talk to the forest,
we will know that the change has come."
— Andrew Joe, Skagit Tribe, Washington

We'll notice first they've quit turning their ears
To catch our voices drifting through cage-bars,
The whites of their eyes no longer shining from corners:
And all dumb animals suddenly struck dumb
Will turn away, embarrassed by a change
Among our hoots and catcalls, whistles and snorts
That crowd the air as tightly as ground-mist.

The cassowary pacing the hurricane fence,
The owl on the driftwood, the gorilla with folding arms,
The buffalo aimed all day in one direction,
The bear on his rock—will need no talking to,
Spending their time so deeply wrapped in time
(Where words lie down like the lion and the lamb)
Not even their own language could reach them.

And so, we'll have to get out of the zoo
To the forest, rain or shine, whichever comes
Dropping its downright shafts before our eyes,
And think of something to say, using new words
That won't turn back bewildered, lost or scattered
Or panicked, curling under the first bush
To wait for a loud voice to hunt them out,

Not words that fall from the skin looking like water
And running together, meaning anything,
Then disappearing into the forest floor
Through gray-green moss and ferns rotting in shade,
Not words like crown-fire overhead, but words
Like old trees felled by themselves in the wilderness,
Making no noise unless someone is listening.

Looking for Mountain Beavers

The man in the feed store called them mountain beavers
When I asked about the burrows riddling the slope
Behind our house. "Sometimes you see dirt moving,

But nothing else," he said. "They eat at night.
My tomcat ate one once, and now he's missing."
He gummed his snuff like a liar. "One ate *him*."

That night my wife and I, carrying flashlights,
Went up the hill to look through brush and bracken
Under the crossfire of the moon for beavers

And, keeping quiet, knelt at pairs of holes
And shone our lights as far as we could reach
Down the smooth runways, finding nothing home,

No brown bushwacker's prints straddling a cat's paw,
Not even each other's lights around the corners.
We ground our heels then, bouncing on the mounds,

Hoping to make one mad enough to exist,
But nothing came out. Should we believe in nothing?
Maybe the cat just dreamed it was eating something

And turned against the nearest raw material
Till its own bones were curled up in its head
Which then fell smiling down a hole and died.

Or maybe the man meant the holes were the beavers:
The deeper they go, the less there is to see.
We felt the earth dip under us now and then

Through no fault of its own, shifting our ground.
But seeing isn't believing: it's disappearing.
All animals are missing—or will be.

Something was eating us. We thumped their houses,
Then walked downhill together, swinging our flashlights
Up and around our heads like holes in the night.

Fragment for a Bulletin Board

Oh God the Founder of our Unreal Estate,
Unwinder of Watchmen, Inspector of Eyelids,
Our Indirect Fluorescence neutral as walls,
Eraser, swift Dispatcher, Lifter of Shades,
Redeemer of all Internal Revenue,
Old Canceller of Checks and Balances,
Keeper of Petty Cash, Unmaker of Memos,
Dispenser of Duplicates, our Perfect Copy . . . .

An Afternoon on the Ground

The ducks and the green drakes
Covered flooded fields.
The herons struck themselves
Aslant in the flowing moss,
And pinetrees, burnt with crows,
Stood short of the mountains.
One hawk rose through the sun,
Casting no shadow down.

These thoughts were five miles long,
Stretched on a river road
Over a frail bridge
Past swampland and meadow
To the prison's honor farm
Where, ghost-pale to the waist,
Running in bare feet,
The trusties were playing ball.

How could I hold them all
Between the sides of my head?
The ducks were as good as gone,
The river would calm down,
The frogs and herons would fly
Together or separately
Like water through the air
Or air over the water,
And the crows all scatter
And the mountain behind them
Be a mountain in a poem
Off which nothing could fall,
And the hawk turn into feathers.

Along that stretch of river
For five miles, hanging on
To the truth of the matter
That led from birds to men,
I had trailed it after me.
But suddenly it tightened.
The end slipped out of my mind,
And the bare-backed prisoners
Were running around a field
On the first good day of spring,
Lifting their arms and shouting.

Walking in the Snow

"...if the author had said, 'Let us put on appropriate galoshes,' there could, of course, have been no poem..."
— an analysis of Elinor Wylie's "Velvet Shoes,"
College English, March 1948, p. 319.

Let us put on appropriate galoshes, letting them flap open,
And walk in the snow.
The eyes have fallen out of the nearest snowman;
It slumps in its shadow,
And the slush at the curb is gray as the breasts of gulls.
As we slog together
Past arbors and stiff trees, all knocked out cold
At the broken end of winter,
No matter what may be falling out of the sky
Or blowing sideways
Against our hearts, we'll make up our own weather.
Love, stamping our galoshes,
Let's say something inappropriate, something flat
As a scholar's ear
And, since this can't be a poem, something loud
And pointless, leading nowhere
Like our footprints ducking and draking in the snow
One after the other.

Sleeping by a River

My feet cut off from me, the ends of my legs
As heavy as the stones they're lying on,
One hand cupped empty over my forehead,
I wake by the riverside, catching myself
Napping, open-mouthed under a cloud.

A rock stuck in my back like a revolver
Holds me up a moment, lets me down
To this numb heap of matter
Whose pieces won't rouse out. I should have known
Better than this. There isn't one dumb creature

Back in the woods who'd fall asleep out here.
There's too much give and take out in the open.
Someone moved the sun when I wasn't looking
And did me to a turn as red as leaves.
Here come the flies across the hatch of evening.

And something drank my spirits while I slept,
Then corked me like a bottle without a message.
It coaxed the soul out of my fingertips,
Spun out its prints as vaguely as whirlpools,
Rippled across my forehead, and flew off.

I shift my upper eye to see the crows
Leaving an alder, full of their dark selves.
This is the way it goes.
The soul goes straight away as the crow flies
With enough noise to wake what's left behind
And leave it, one eye up, like a dying salmon.

After Falling

Sleep lightly, sleep eventfully
That from the jangling backs of your eyes may come the harness
Without horses, the trappings of darkness
And a country in pieces wedged across pale hills
And out of the mind—through fields ragged with light
Where the wrong birds out of season
Crouch in the grass, their wings trembling like eyelids.

Sleep watchfully, now, leaning across
The long strands holding the night like reins through clouds
And darkening with them, flourishing into water
Where the rough road divides repeatedly,
Dissolving slowly, streaming over the ground
But springing again, as the birds will,
To climb through wilder country before falling.

Burying a Weasel

He was still moving
When I prodded him off the highway onto a plank
And into my yard. I set him down and touched him.
Now, because I still have all my fingers
(Trappers told it this way to kings)
I know he's dead.

Cat whiskers, translucent claws,
The tawny shades dividing back and belly,
Tail dipped in black,
And the lithe deadlines — being a weasel
Doesn't end at that. An old man told me
One jumped into a moose's ear and never came out.

He'd have had a robin's egg by now, tipping the goblet
Down his experienced, wild throat
Which I smooth without quite daring to.
Instead, he has his own blood in his mouth,
Grudging each drop
That gets away into the earth.

He knew what to be in burrows dug by others
And will do it again under my shovel
Out of his nature. Grass crosses highways too,
Having been run over somewhere
By every conceivable shape.
My pasture was invented for dead animals.

A Valedictory to Standard Oil of Indiana

In the darkness east of Chicago, the sky burns over the
  plumbers' nightmares
Red and blue, and my hometown lies there loaded with
  gasoline.
Registers ring like gas-pumps, pumps like pinballs, pinballs like
  broken alarm clocks,
And it's time for morning, but nothing's going to work.
From cat-cracker to candle-shop, from grease-works along the
  pipeline,
Over storage tanks like kings on a checkerboard ready to jump
  the county,
The word goes out: With refined regrets
We suggest you sleep all day in your houses shaped like lunch
  buckets
And don't show up at the automated gates.
Something else will tap the gauges without yawning
And check the valves at the feet of the cooling-towers without
  complaining.

Standard Oil is canning my high school classmates
And the ones who fell out of junior high or slipped in the grades.
What should they do, gassed up in their Tempests and Comets,
  raring to go
Somewhere with their wives scowling in front and kids stuffed
  in the back,
Past drive-ins jammed like car-lots, trying to find the beaches
But blocked by freights for hours, stopped dead in their tracks
Where the rails, as thick as thieves along the lakefront,
Lower their crossing gates to shut the frontier? What can they
  think about
As they stare at the sides of boxcars for a sign,
And Lake Michigan drains slowly into Lake Huron,
The mills level the Dunes, and the eels go sailing through the
  trout,

[44]

And mosquitoes inherit the evening, while toads no bigger than horseflies
Hop crazily after them over the lawns and sidewalks, and the rainbows fall
Flat in the oil they came from? There are two towns now,
One dark, one going to be dark, divided by cyclone fences;
One pampered and cared for like pillboxes and cathedrals,
The other vanishing overnight in the dumps and swamps like a struck sideshow.
As the Laureate of the Class of '44 — which doesn't know it has one —
I offer this poem, not from hustings or barricades
Or the rickety stage where George Rogers Clark stood glued to the wall,
But from another way out, like Barnum's "This Way to the Egress,"
Which moved the suckers when they'd seen enough. Get out of town.

Morning Song

Once dark together, now we're turning white.
The colorless music in the leaves shakes downward.
We trace the sheet from there, to there, to here.
It dawns on us that we must come apart.

The air is tilting at the windowsills.
The crossbones of our elbows are chilled white.
The sun and the moon cross over separate walls.
The quick is sinking in our fingernails.

Bleak morning leaches out the soles of our feet.
Our teeth are shining under open eyes.
Even the lilies' anthers have gone white.
The first thin stretch of milk has skimmed the stairs.

Our cottony mouths are flocked with silence now.
Light on our foreheads flutters like blown paper.
The gauzy ceiling stiffens into plaster.
Our lips together put their white on white.

The dust like frost is bristling on the floor.
Daylight rolls over in its bed of ashes.
And far too much of a good thing in the sky
Is beaming down as pale as a marble angel.

Not mattering, our matter has turned white.

The Circuit

My circuit-riding great-grandfather
Rode off on horseback through the hickory woods
Each week to galvanize five Methodist churches,
And once, passing a Sabbath-breaking auction,
Shouted over his shoulder, "Fifteen cents!"
They caught him miles away
And saddled him with an old grandfather clock.

What got you up on your horse in the morning, sir?
Did you rehearse damnation
Till the trees fell crossways like a corduroy road?
Did anyone catch his death, as you caught yours,
Coming to hear you freezing in a shed?
Nobody mentions anything you did
Except the clock—no name-dropping of God,
No chiming adage. A joke thrown back of a horse
Has lasted longer than your rules and reasons.

I saw you stiff as a tintype in your bed
Next to a basin and a worn-out Bible,
Your beard aimed at the ceiling like a sermon.
Over the distance I can hear you shouting,
"Where in the name of God is the Name of God
In all these damned unsingable useless poems?"

Your family fought harder for the clock
Than they did for souls, and now they know its face
Better than yours, having replaced the works.
Beards are no longer hanging out of pulpits;
If God speaks from a bush, it's only by chance.
I shave my face and wait,
But bid for every clock I lay my eyes on
Just for the hell of it, your Hell and mine.
Like you, I'm doing time in the hard woods,
Tracking myself in circles, a lost preacher.

Speech from a Comedy

(Scene: The wreckage of Heaven)

I am God. But all my creatures are unkind to me.
They think of themselves. Why don't they think of me?
I'm holier than they.
    (Chorus) God is lovely.
If I descended and rode through the streets,
Would they take off their hats?
No, they'd keep their hands in each other's pockets.
    (Chorus) God is out of sorts.
Or if I showed up to give a formal address
Including an enormous amount of sound, godly advice,
They'd turn and wriggle away like a school of fish.
    (Chorus) God is endless.
I burned myself in a bush once. Day and night,
I burned like a pillar of virtue in the desert.
I even let them watch me ride in my chariot.
    (Chorus) God is great.
I gave them Aaron's rod when they were on the rocks.
I plagued their enemies with a thousand dirty tricks.
I let them burn rams in thickets instead of their precious Issacs.
    (Chorus) God is on their backs.
When things looked so black they couldn't tell his from hers,
I parted the waters,
Saving a few. But drowning a lot of others.
    (Chorus) God is feeling worse.
Didn't I die for them?
Hang myself? And shed the Blood of the Lamb?
What more could I do? Try it yourself sometime.
    (Chorus) God is sublime.
Now they forsake me. Leave me up in the air.
Sinning. Thinking of pleasure.
The more I leave them alone, the worse they are.
    (Chorus) God is pure.
They lie all night in their houses stacked in rows,

Their knees pulled up, their heads stuffed into pillows,
Imagining new ways to break my laws.
> *(Chorus)* God is jealous.

When I show them a bad example, plastered and confused,
Chances are he'll be headlined and idolized.
The only law of mine they like is getting circumcized.
> *(Chorus)* God is not amused.

I didn't ask for anything impossible.
I said, "Love me—and not just once in a while."
But all men were created fickle.
> *(Chorus)* God is immortal.

I'll settle with Everyman.
I had his dinner all laid out in my mansion,
But *he* had to try cooking his *own*.
> *(Chorus)* God is burning.

Just because angels are blasé and neuter,
Did he think I'd be contented forever and ever
Playing with Ezekiel's wheel or climbing up and down
  Jacob's ladder?
> *(Chorus)* God is boiling over.

I made him in my image, didn't I?
I gave him my tooth for a tooth, my eye for an eye.
How could I turn out such an unreasonable facsimile?
> *(Chorus)* God is mighty sorry.

He'll be made to see the way things really are.
If he's so fond of slaughter,
I can get it for him wholesale just by losing my temper.
> *(Chorus)* God's a man-of-war.

I might have shown him mercy,
But nobody asked me.
The best things in Heaven are costly.
> *(Chorus)* God is free.

All right, he's dug his bed. Now let him lie in it
A thousand years at a stretch on a strict diet
While worms with their noses on fire pay an endless visit.
> *(Chorus)* God is like that.

I watched over him like a shepherd over a sheep
While he went bleating and gambolling and flocking around
    and getting fleeced, forgetting whom to worship.
Well, every shepherd knows his way to the butchershop.
    (Chorus) God is in bad shape.
Come, Death. He has made me mad.
I summon Death. For his ingratitude,
Everyman must choke on his daily bread.
    (Chorus) God is sick and tired.

The Osprey's Nest

The osprey's nest has dropped of its own weight
After years, breaking everything under it, collapsing
Out of the sky like the wreckage of the moon,
Having killed its branch and rotted its lodgepole:
A flying cloud of fishbones tall as a man,
A shambles of dead storms ten feet across.

Uncertain what holds anything together,
Ospreys try everything—fishnets and broomsticks,
Welcome-mats and pieces of scarecrows,
Sheep bones, shells, the folded wings of mallards—
And heap up generations till they topple.

In the nest the young ones, calling fish to fly
Over the water toward them in old talons,
Thought only of hunger diving down their throats
To the heart, not letting go—(not letting go,
Ospreys have washed ashore, ruffled and calm
But drowned, their claws embedded in salmon).
They saw the world was bones and curtain-rods,
Hay-wire and cornstalks—rubble put to bed
And glued into meaning by large appetites.
Living on top of everything that mattered,
The fledglings held it in the air with their eyes,
With awkward claws groping the ghosts of fish.

Last night they slapped themselves into the wind
And cried across the rain, flopping for comfort
Against the nearest branches, baffled by leaves
And the blank darkness falling below their breasts.
Where have they gone? The nest, now heaped on the bank,
Has come to earth smelling as high as heaven.

Near the End of the Party

The party, spilling slowly over the terrace
Along the steps, is running down the garden
Onto the lawn—men taking a little something
With them for luck against the growing night
Behind their backs, the women following,
Their heads nodding like roses over roses.

The plots laid out in the dark in all directions
Go on past winning and losing arguments.
Hazy together, lips run out of words.
The grass is yielding gracefully underfoot.
And slipping sideways, straight from the shoulder now,
The vaguest necklines take the plunge to heart,

And the first to pour himself out on the ground
Is lying still as a perennial border.
The sprinkler, like a melting chandelier,
Spins on itself and darkens. Under the wind,
Over and over like the ghosts of moles,
The napkins tumble through the flowerbeds.

Observations from the Outer Edge

I pass the abrupt end of the woods, and stop.
I'm standing on a cliff as sheer as a step
Where the ground, like the ground floor of a nightmare,
Has slipped a notch six hundred rocky feet
And left itself in the lurch. My shoes go dead.
Not looking yet, I let my heart sneak back,

But feel like the fall-guy ending a Western,
The heavy, bound to topple from the edge
And disappear with terrible gravity.
I put my hand out in the separate air
With nothing under it, but it feels nothing.
This is no place for putting my foot down,

So I shout my name, but can't scare up an echo.
No one inside this canyon wants to be me.
I manage to look down. Not much to envy:
The silent, immobile rapids, the toy pines,
A fisherman stuck in the shallows like an agate—
A world so far away, it could quit moving

And I wouldn't know the difference. I've seen it before
At the ends of hallways, the far sides of windows,
Shrinking from sight. Down is no worse than across.
Whether it's sky, horizon, or ground zero,
A piece of space will take whatever comes
From any direction—climbing, walking, or falling.

I remember a newsreel—a man holding a baby
Over the Grand Canyon on a stick:
The kid hung on and grinned for the camera.
I grab the nearest branch just to make sure
It isn't death down there, looking like hell.
Even a mountain goat will go to pieces

Standing on glass suspended in the air,
But man created with a jerkier balance
Can learn to fix his eyes on a safe place.
Trembling somewhere,
The acrophobiac Primum Mobile
Clings to his starry axle, staring sideways.

Making Up for a Soul

It's been like fixing a clock, jamming the wheels,
The pinions, and bent springs into a box
And shaking it. Or like patching a vase,
Gluing the mismatched edges of events
Together despite the quirks in the design.
Or trying to make one out of scraps of paper,
The yellowing, dog-eared pages going slapdash
Over each other, flat as a collage.
I can't keep time with it. It won't hold water.
Ripping and rearranging make no pattern.

Imagine me with a soul: I'm sitting here
In the room with you, smiling from corner to corner,
My chest going up and down with inspiration.
I sit serene, insufferably at my ease,
Not scratching or drumming but merely suffering
Your questions, like the man from the back of the book
With all the answers. You couldn't stand me, could you?

My love, if *you* have a soul, don't tell me yet.
Why can't we simply stay uneasy together?
There are snap-on souls like luminous neckties
That light up in the dark, spelling our names.
Let's put them on for solemn visitors,
Switch off the lights, then grope from room to room,
Making our hollow, diabolical noises
Like Dracula and his spouse, avoiding mirrors,
Clutching each other fiendishly for life
To stop the gaps in ourselves, like better halves.

Leaving Something Behind

A fox at your neck and snakeskin on your feet,
You have gone to the city behind an ivory brooch,
Wearing your charms for and against desire, bearing your
    beauty
Past all the gaping doorways, amazing women on edge
And leading men's eyes astray while skirting mayhem,
And I, for a day, must wish you safe in your skin.

The diggers named her the Minnesota Girl. She was fifteen,
Eight thousand years ago, when she drowned in a glacial lake,
Curling to sleep like her sea-snail amulet, holding a turtleshell,
A wolf's tooth, the tine of an antler, carrying somehow
A dozen bones from the feet of water birds. She believed in her
    charms,
But something found her and kept her. She became what she
    wore.

She loved her bones and her own husk of creatures
But left them piecemeal on the branching shore.
Without you, fox paws, elephant haunches, all rattling tails,
Snails' feet, turtles' remote hearts, muzzles of wolves,
Stags' ears, and the tongues of water birds are only themselves.
Come safely back. There was nothing in her arms.

Working Against Time

By the newly bulldozed logging road, for a hundred yards,
I saw the sprawling five-foot hemlocks, their branches crammed
Into each other's light, upended or wrenched aslant
Or broken across waists the size of broomsticks
Or bent, crushed slewfoot on themselves in the duff like briars,
Their roots coming at random out of the dirt, and dying.

I had no burlap in the trunk, not even a spade,
And the shirt off my back wasn't enough to go around.
I'm no tree surgeon, it wasn't Arbor Day, but I climbed
Over the free-for-all, untangling winners and losers
And squeezing as many as I could into my car.
When I started, nothing was singing in the woods except me.

I hardly had room to steer — roots dangled over my shoulder
And scraped the side of my throat as if looking for water.
Branches against the fog on the windshield dabbled designs
Like kids or hung out the vent. The sun was falling down.
It's against the law to dig up trees. Working against
Time and across laws, I drove my ambulance

Forty miles in the dark to the house and began digging
Knee-deep graves for most of them, while the splayed headlights
Along the highway picked me out of the night:
A fool with a shovel searching for worms or treasure,
Both buried behind the sweat on his forehead. Two green
    survivors
Are tangled under the biting rain as I say this.

A Room with a View

1

At last, outside my window an expanse
For the mind's elbows, stretching north and south:
Houseboats and towers, drydocks and seaplanes,
Streets vaulting over hillsides
And the top of the sky pushed backward through the clouds,
Then over high bridges into the distance
Where the sun is breaking, falling beyond the mountains.

In the darkness, blazing like campfires locked in glass,
The lights from other houses
Survive the invisible weather of the night.
I watch through the dawn
Cars butting each other down long chutes to the city
And the black-decked seiner circling the inlet,
Dragging its purse behind, then slewing away
With the morning offering, leaving the water empty.

2

Looking up from a book or half a sentence
For some way out, I've seen from other rooms
Weeds sloping up to brambles, telephone wires,
Or strips of grass like runners between neighbors,
Or only the sweating windows
Themselves, as blank as paper, or streaky shades
Like moths too big and battered to get out.

Now the reach and stretch of this astounding air
Unfocuses my eyes. Whatever is coming
Must come from as far away as the horizon.
To see what I could only imagine once
When, shut in a box, I heard hard winter knocking,
Makes me afraid. Having set myself to think,
Having arranged to watch the weather coming,

I'm afraid it won't be real:
The wind in a single lane, the clouds in rows,
The lightning mastered in an orderly sheaf,
The snow and sleet in clusters,
The uniform thunder rolling itself flat.

A man in a room with a view draws back—
As though on a cliff—from the edge of the operatic,
Tempted to own it, to get above himself.
Poets and *helden* tenors, straining for height,
Mistake the roaring in their ears for the ocean.

3
In a small glass box I've made a terrarium:
Eight kinds of moss from the banks of mountain streams
Whose interlacing fern-like leaves
And outflung sporophytes like spears in a mob-scene
Make perfect sense from only a foot away,
As unpredictably various as a shrine
In a Zen garden, or a piece of forest floor
Where every inch of the dead is crammed with blossoms.

If I grew tired as a god and forgot its water
Or dumped it out the window
Or set out scientifically to destroy it
By fire or drowning or some kind of mayhem,
The least fragment, a half-burnt speck or spore
Or the most unlikely single rootless cell,
Where the green goes dark as night, could breed again
An entire garden. Here, pressed against the glass
On four high sides like the corners of the world,
It breathes my breath. Its weather is my face.

Running

Running across country easily at evening, taking the stones
As easily as stubble, running from nothing but going
Past fences swamped by berries, into a high field
And down a long furrow sloping into wheat, then climbing
To scatter the booming pheasants, crossing and turning
Where cinders slant to a bridge, then underneath
And down a green creekbank over the crowns of logs
Through shallow water and ferns, stumbling into the woods
To a clearing gold as a haystack, faltering
Now, breath going back, and forth, catching
And breaking, then running down to the ground
To a deeper grassbank, sprawling, raking the air
And sweating it out, a stretch of sky thrown backward,
Blinking, scraping at breath
As brokenly as heart-beats, everything in the rib-cage running
And running, going ahead
Without me across country, the deep breath burning.

Come Before His Countenance with a Joyful Leaping

Swivelling flat-soled on the dirt but ready to bound in arches
        at the nick of time, spurring yourselves, come all as
        you are with footbones rattling like claques, with
        storking knees careering into the crooked distance,
        horning in and out of sight,
Come coasting in circles, rearing, running aground, and
        flickering up the air, peeling and flaking away like
        handbills over the sloping daylight,
Come lambing and fishing, outflanking the body's heights at a
        single stroke, out of breath, out at the elbows,
        spreading blank palms and flinching up hillsides
        hoisted out of mind,
Come at a loss out of manholes and sandtraps, jerking free at
        the heart, assaulted and blinking on dislocated ankles,
        swollen with song from the twisted wreckage, dying
        and rigorous after the second wind,
For He is falling apart in His unstrung parbuckles, His beard
        blown loose by harmonious unction, His countenance
        breaking, His fragments flopping up and around
        without us to the stretches of morning.

Song to Accompany
the Bearer of Bad News

Kings kill their messengers
Sometimes, slicing wildly
Through pages delivering their grief
And you may do the same
With this page under this poem
Tear it lengthwise first
With feeling, cutting off
Each phrase into meaningless halves
Then crossways, severing
The mild beginning from the bad ending
By now you know the worst
Having imagined the remainder
Down to the painful inch
Where something like your name
Closes this message
You needn't finish now
You may stop here
And puzzle it out later.

Kings kill
Sometimes, slicing
Through pages
And you may
With this page
Tear it
With feeling
Each phrase
Then crossways
The mild beginning
By now you know
Having imagined
Down to
Where something

Closes
You needn't finish
You may stop
And puzzle it out.

Their messengers
Wildly
Delivering their grief
Do the same
Under this poem
Lengthwise first
Cutting off
Into meaningless halves
Severing
The bad ending
The worst
The remainder
The painful inch
Like your name
This message
Now
Here
Later

You may   tear it   into meaningless halves
Lengthwise first   then crossways
Severing   something like   the painful inch
Later   under this poem   messengers
Delivering their grief   puzzle it out
Having imagined   the worst
Kings kill   wildly   through pages
Cutting off   the bad ending
Do the same   with this page
By now you know   the mild beginning
Down to where   your name   closes
With feeling   now   you may stop.